OUR GALAXY AND BEYOND

MARS

By Darlene R. Stille

The Child's World®

Published in the United States of America by The Child's World®
P.O. Box 326, Chanhassen, MN 55317-0326
800-599-READ
www.childsworld.com

Content Adviser:
Michelle Nichols,
Lead Educator for
Informal Programs,
Adler Planetarium
& Astronomy
Museum, Chicago,
Illinois

The Child's World®: Mary Berendes, Publishing Director
Editorial Directions, Inc.: E. Russell Primm, Editorial Director; Dana Rau, Line
Editor; Elizabeth K. Martin, Assistant Editor; Olivia Nellums, Editorial Assistant;
Susan Hindman, Copy Editor; Susan Ashley, Proofreader; Kevin Cunningham,
Peter Garnham, Chris Simms, Fact Checkers; Tim Griffin/IndexServ, Indexer;
Cian Loughlin O'Day, Photo Researcher; Linda S. Koutris, Photo Selector

Library of Congress Cataloging-in-Publication Data
Stille, Darlene R.
 Mars / by Darlene Stille.
  p. cm. — (Our galaxy and beyond)
Summary: Introduces the planet Mars, exploring its atmosphere, composition,
and other characteristics and looking particularly at how humans learned about the
only planet that can be seen clearly from Earth. Includes bibliographical references
and index.
 ISBN 1-59296-050-2 (lib. bdg. : alk. paper)
 1. Mars (Planet)—Juvenile literature. [1. Mars (Planet)] I. Title. II. Series.
 QB641.S74 2004
 523.43—dc21   2003006331

TABLE OF CONTENTS

CHAPTER ONE

DISCOVERING MARS

No one knows who first saw the planet Mars. The earliest people on Earth probably knew about Mars. They saw it as a red dot in the sky. We can often see Mars clearly from Earth even without **telescopes.**

Mars is one of the nine planets in our solar system that orbit, or go around, the Sun. It is the fourth planet from the Sun. Mars was named after the Roman god of war. Maybe this name was chosen because red is the color of blood. Mars is also nicknamed the Red Planet.

After telescopes were invented, **astronomers** made many discoveries about Mars. In the 1700s, they saw dark areas on Mars that they thought were seas. In 1877, American astronomer Asaph

Mars, the Roman God of War, was famed for riding the battlefield in his chariot, changing the outcome of a war.

Hall discovered two moons orbiting Mars. He named the moons

Phobos and Deimos. That same year, an Italian astronomer named

Giovanni V. Schiaparelli reported seeing strange lines on Mars. Some

scientists thought the lines were canals, or big waterways dug by

people. They thought there must be people or other life-forms on

Mars who had dug these canals.

An engineer works with the model of the Viking *lander.*

In 1965, the National Aeronautics and Space Administration (NASA) sent the first spacecraft to Mars. The spacecraft was a space **probe** named *Mariner 4.* It did not carry people, but it did carry cameras. *Mariner 4* flew close to Mars and began taking pictures. The pictures cleared up one mystery. They showed that there are no canals on Mars. After that first probe, the United States and the Soviet Union (now Russia) sent several more space probes to Mars. Some even landed on the planet.

In 1976, the United States sent out two space probes called *Viking 1* and *Viking 2.* Part of the spacecraft, called landers, landed on the surface of Mars. Their cameras showed astronomers the red rocks and soil of Mars as if they were right there. In 1996, NASA sent another

Photographs taken from the Viking 2 *probe provided scientists with a good look at the dusty, rocky Martian landscape.*

lander, called *Mars Pathfinder,* and a small robot rover called *Sojourner.* The rover moved around to study the surface of Mars.

NASA sent two orbiting spacecraft to Mars after *Pathfinder.* The Hubble Space Telescope, in orbit high above Earth, has also studied Mars. Scientists now have a very good idea of what Mars is like.

WAR OF THE WORLDS

On October 30, 1938, Americans turned on their radios and heard some terrifying news. Martians were invading Earth! Their spaceships were landing in New Jersey. Many people believed the news. After all, at that time some people still thought Mars had canals that were dug by intelligent beings. They panicked. Some people in and around New Jersey started packing their cars to flee the invaders. They soon discovered that it was just a Halloween prank, a radio show put on by an actor named Orson Welles. The plot of the show came from a science fiction novel called *The War of the Worlds,* by the English author H. G. Wells. The radio show made it sound like reporters were on the scene telling about the invasion. Orson Welles was surprised at how people behaved. They had really believed that a Martian invasion was possible!

CHAPTER TWO

MARS'S ATMOSPHERE

If you could stand on Mars and look up at the sky, you would probably see clouds. You might see pink clouds made of dust. You might see blue clouds made of ice crystals. You might see white

If you visited Mars you might see these twin peaks in the distance.
Both of these small hills are under 100 feet (30.5 meters) high.

clouds made of water vapor. When water is heated, it turns into a gas called water vapor.

But you would not be able to breathe. That is because the atmosphere around Mars is very different from Earth's atmosphere. An atmosphere is the layer of gases that surrounds a planet. The atmosphere of Mars is very thin. There is very little oxygen in the Martian atmosphere. Oxygen is the gas people need to breathe in order to live. Most of the gas in the atmosphere of Mars is carbon dioxide. This is the gas that animal life on Earth breathes out.

There are seasons on Mars just as there are on Earth. This is because Mars is tilted a little on its axis. An axis is the imaginary line going through the very top and bottom, or poles, of a planet. The tilt of an axis gives a planet seasons. But it would be hard to keep warm on Mars during any season. Even on a warm summer day, the temperature usually does not go higher than 32° Fahrenheit (0° Celsius). That is the freezing point of water on Earth. It is even colder at the far north and south poles of Mars. It can be as cold as −225° F (−143° C) at the poles in winter.

Scientists are able to track the weather patterns across Mars by taking pictures of the planet over time and comparing the pictures with each other.

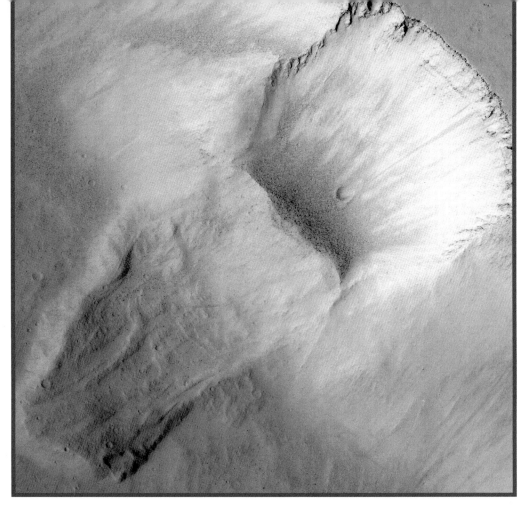

Mars has very rugged terrain, or land. The Mars Global Surveyor took this image of a landslide in a Martian valley.

The weather on Mars is wild. Huge dust storms form during summer in the southern half of Mars. Some dust storms grow so big that they cover almost the entire planet. There are also small dust devils on Mars. Dust devils are whirling winds that pick up bits of soil.

CHAPTER THREE

WHAT MARS IS MADE OF

If you could take a trip around Mars, you would see that about two-thirds of the planet is covered with reddish-brown sand dunes. Orbiting spacecraft have made a map of Mars. The map shows that Mars has highlands and lowlands. The highlands are raised areas. They are in the southern part of Mars. The lowlands are lower areas in the northern half of the planet. Scientists wonder if the raised areas on Mars are like the large landmasses we call continents on Earth. They wonder if the lowlands are like the bottoms of lakes or oceans.

The southern highland area looks like Earth's Moon. It has many craters. The craters were made by **meteorites** crashing into the planet about four billion years ago. The meteorites must

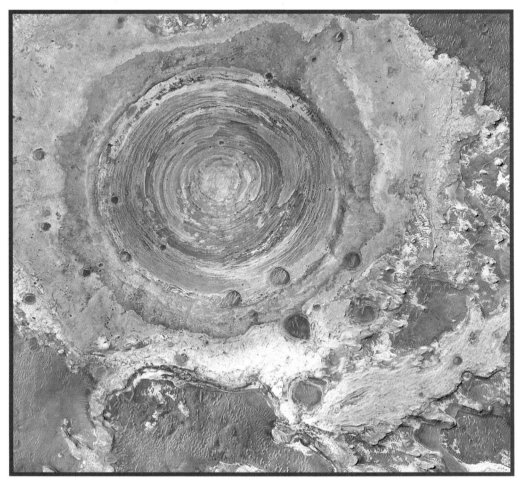

This crater on Mars was created long ago by a meteorite.

have been very large. Some of the craters are hundreds of miles

across. The lowlands have fewer craters. The lowlands are more like

smooth plains.

There is a smaller raised area in the northern half of the planet.

It is called the Tharsis Bulge. It is about twice the size of the United

States. The biggest **volcanoes** of Mars are on the Tharsis Bulge.

The largest volcano is called Olympus Mons, which means Mount

Olympus. It rises up 16 miles (25 kilometers) from the surface of

Mars. That makes it the biggest mountain in the solar system. It is

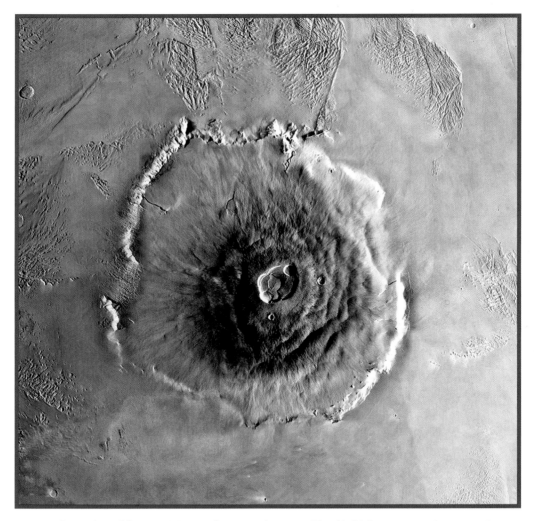

Mars's massive Olympus Mons volcano makes even Earth's highest mountains seem tiny.

three times taller than Mount Everest, the highest mountain on Earth. The bottom, or base, of Olympus Mons is as big as the whole state of Arizona!

The equator is an imaginary line running around the middle of a planet. Along the equator of Mars is a huge canyon called Valles Marineris, or Mariner Valley. This canyon is about 2,500 miles (4,000 km) long. Valles Marineris would stretch across the entire United States. In some places, it is up to 4 miles (6.4 km) deep. The Grand Canyon in the United States is only about 1 mile (1.6 km) deep.

There are ice caps at the north and south poles. The ice is made of frozen water and frozen carbon dioxide. Frozen carbon dioxide is called dry ice. The ice caps on Mars grow bigger in the winter. They shrink or disappear in summer.

Scientists now think that Mars either has a core, or center, made

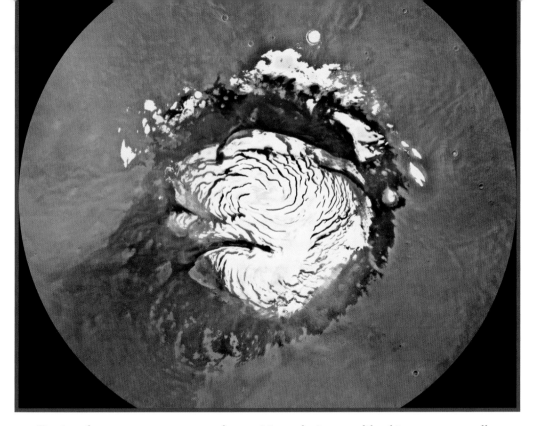

During the warmer summer weather on Mars, the ice caps like this one grow smaller.

of liquid iron or a liquid outer core and a solid inner core. Above the core is a layer of melted rock called the mantle. On top of the mantle is the surface, or crust, of Mars. Wide channels and deep gullies criss-cross the surface. They look like dried riverbeds. On Earth, gullies and channels are cuts through the land, usually created by rushing water such as rivers. But Mars doesn't seem to have any water. So how were these landforms created?

Many scientists think that the best way to explore Mars is by using robot rovers. A robot rover can travel around. It can take pictures and study rocks and soil. The first robot rover to land on Mars was *Sojourner*. *Sojourner* arrived on *Mars Pathfinder,* a spacecraft that was unmanned, meaning that it carried no people. *Pathfinder* landed on Mars on July 4, 1997. *Sojourner* rolled out of *Pathfinder* and down a ramp to the surface of Mars. *Sojourner* was about the size of a toy wagon. It rolled on wheels. It carried cameras and instruments for studying Mars. People on Earth used remote-control radio commands to tell *Sojourner* where to go.

NASA scientists are making better robot rovers. They are testing them in a place that looks like Mars. They call it a Marscape. Marscape covers about three-quarters of an acre in California. It has a meteorite crater, a dry lake bed, a channel that looks like it was carved by water, and jumbles of rocks. Robots called K9 rovers go through tests at the Marscape. A K9 rover runs on six wheels, carries cameras, and gets its power from the sun. "Our goal," says a NASA computer engineer, "is to have a 'smart robot' that we can send off to Mars in 2009 that will take care of itself."

CHAPTER FOUR

THE GREAT MARTIAN WATER MYSTERY

Scientists think there was once water on Mars. The canyons and gullies look like they were dug out by flowing water. Yet all the spacecraft sent to Mars have found that the planet is very dry.

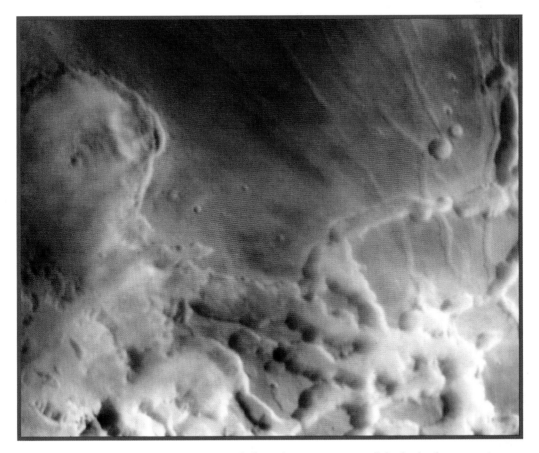

Bright ice clouds are seen here around the tributary canyons of the high plateau region of Mars. These canyons may have been formed by water.

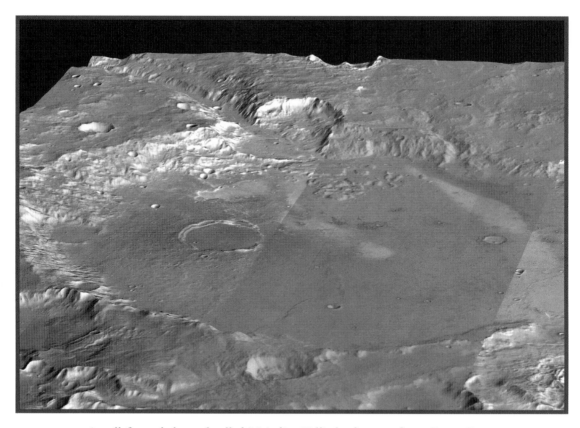

A well-formed channel called Ma'adim Vallis leads away from Gusev Crater, which some scientists believe is an ancient lake bed.

Liquid water cannot exist on the surface of Mars today. The temperature is too cold, and the atmosphere is too thin. Water would either freeze or turn into water vapor. So where did the water come from? Where did the water go? These are mysteries that scientists are trying to solve.

Scientists have two ideas about water on Mars. One idea is

that, long ago, Mars had rivers and lakes filled with water. Mars was much warmer then. Something happened to make the planet's surface colder. The water froze or turned to vapor. The water that was left may have gone underground.

This leads to the other idea. Some scientists believe that Mars still has water under its surface. Once in a while, the water bursts out. Rushing water carves gullies. It scatters rocks and boulders all around. Then the water freezes or turns to vapor. Not a trace of liquid water is left behind. A small amount of frozen water has been found underground near one of the poles of Mars. But where the rest of the underground water might be is unknown.

Scientists think it is very important to solve the mystery of the Martian water. If there was once water, there may also have been life on Mars.

CHAPTER FIVE

Searching for Life on Mars

For a long time, people have thought that there might be life on Mars. Some of the spacecraft sent to Mars looked for signs of life. The *Viking* landers had arms that scooped up soil. Instruments in the landers tested the soil. One of the *Viking* probes worked for several years. But it found no signs of life. The *Sojourner* rover also tested the soil. *Sojourner* found nothing that looked like life on Mars.

In 1996, a group of scientists said they might have found signs that there was life on Mars

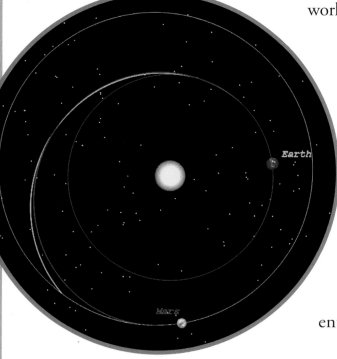

This diagram shows how one of the spacecraft sent to Mars, called the Mars Pathfinder, *entered the Martian atmosphere without going into orbit around the planet.*

These scientists study meteorites from Mars, hoping to find clues to the question of whether or not life has ever existed there.

long ago. They did not find these signs of life on the Red Planet.

Instead, they found them in a meteorite on Earth. The scientists

think the meteorite was a piece of rock blasted off Mars when a

comet hit the planet. The meteorite has tiny tubes that look like

the remains of ancient bacteria. Some scientists think that the

tubes show that bacteria may have lived on Mars billions of years

ago. Other scientists do not believe that this meteorite contains

proof of life. The search for life on Mars continues.

Could human beings live on Mars? Could Mars be made more like Earth? Some scientists have given these questions a lot of thought. And they have some ideas. One involves making the planet more like Earth, a method called terraforming. No one knows if terraforming Mars or any planet or moon can really work.

Scientists believe Mars may be similar to the way Earth was billions of years ago. For example, its thin atmosphere is made mostly of carbon dioxide, just as ancient Earth's was. But Mars is much colder than Earth was. Terraforming Mars would start by adding even more carbon dioxide to the atmosphere to help warm the planet. On Earth, carbon dioxide acts like a greenhouse. It traps heat from the Sun and helps keep Earth warm. This is called the greenhouse effect.

Carbon dioxide would come from the ice caps on Mars. The ice caps are made of water ice and frozen carbon dioxide. Melting the ice caps would make carbon dioxide gas and water. Sprinkling dark Martian dust on the white ice would melt the ice caps. The ice would grow warmer because dark colors take up more heat from the Sun than light colors. The carbon dioxide would rise into the atmosphere and trap heat.

After Mars became warm enough, plants could grow. Trees make food from carbon dioxide, sunlight, and water. Trees give off oxygen when they make food. Someday, Mars would be warm enough and have enough oxygen for people to live there. Terraforming would take hundreds of years—if it worked at all.

CHAPTER SIX

HOW MARS MAY
HAVE FORMED

Mars is one of four rocky planets in our solar system. The other

rocky planets are Mercury, Venus, and Earth. They are called rocky

planets because they have solid surfaces of rocks and soil. Like all the

*A comparison of Mars and Earth shows that, though they are alike in some ways,
there are many differences between the two.*

planets, Mars formed from a cloud of dust and gas about 4.6 billion years ago. The part of the cloud closest to the Sun, where Mars and the other rocky planets formed, had bits of rock and metal. These bits clumped together to form the rocky planets.

Earth and Mars may have been very similar to each other at first. The atmospheres of both planets may have had lots of carbon dioxide. The surface of both planets may have been covered with water.

Earth's atmosphere changed a lot. Today, it has less carbon dioxide and more oxygen. On Mars, the water disappeared. People can live on the surface of Earth, but they cannot live on the surface of Mars. Yet, some scientists still think there may be signs of life somewhere on Mars.

Some scientists would like to send astronauts to look for life on Mars. It would be hard for people to explore Mars. They would have to bring lots of oxygen and water with them. When they went outside, they would have to wear space suits and helmets filled with air to breathe. The space suits would keep them warm and protect them against burning rays from the Sun.

Other scientists think robots are a better way to explore Mars. NASA **engineers** are working on more robot spacecraft to land on Mars. Someday, a spacecraft may return to Earth from Mars. It will bring back samples of rocks and soil.

It will be many years before any human beings can go to Mars. The astronauts who may someday go there are children in school today. So, who knows? Maybe you will be the one who lands on Mars. Maybe you will discover more secrets of the Red Planet. Maybe you will find out once and for all if there has ever been life on Mars.

Glossary

astronomers (uh-STRAW-nuh-merz) Astronomers are scientists who study space and the stars and planets.

comet (KOM-it) A comet is a bright object followed by a tail of dust and ice that orbits the Sun in a long, oval-shaped path.

engineers (en-juh-NIHRS) Engineers are people who design and build machines, bridges, and buildings.

meteorites (MEE-tee-uh-rites) Meteorites are rocky or metallic objects from space that hit the surface of a planet or moon.

probe (PROBE) A probe is a machine or tool that explores something.

telescopes (TEL-uh-skopes) Telescopes are instruments used to study things that are far away, such as stars and planets, by making them seem larger and closer.

volcanoes (vol-KAY-nose) Volcanoes are mountains that contain an opening in the surface of a planet. When a volcano erupts, melted rock from pools of magma below the surface spews from the top.

Did You Know?

▶ Mars looks red because there is rust in the soil. Rust is made of iron and oxygen. Long ago, iron on the surface of Mars combined with oxygen in its atmosphere. This action made rust.

▶ Phobos and Deimos, the two small moons of Mars, are shaped like potatoes. They may once have been asteroids, chunks of rock that orbit the Sun. There are many asteroids between Mars and Jupiter. Phobos and Deimos may have been two of those asteroids until they were captured by the gravity of Mars. Gravity is the force that attracts a small object to a larger one.

▶ The seasons on Mars are twice as long as the seasons on Earth. This is because Mars is farther from the Sun than Earth. It takes Mars twice as long to orbit around the Sun.

▶ A Martian day is called a sol. In Earth time, there are 24 hours and 40 minutes in a sol. A year is the time it takes a planet to go around the Sun once. A Martian-year is 669 sols. A year on Mars is about 10 $\frac{1}{2}$ months longer than a year on Earth.

▶ A huge crater named Hellas in the southern highlands of Mars is 6 miles (9 km) deep and 1,300 miles (2,100 km) across.

Fast Facts

Diameter: 4,222 miles (6,794 kilometers)

Atmosphere: carbon dioxide, nitrogen, argon, oxygen, carbon monoxide, neon, krypton, xenon, and water vapor

Time to orbit the Sun (one Mars-year): 687 Earth-days

Time to turn on axis (one Mars-day): 24.6 Earth-hours

Shortest distance from the Sun: 130 million miles (207 million km)

Greatest distance from the Sun: 155 million miles (250 million km)

Shortest distance from Earth: 34.6 million miles (55.7 million km)

Greatest distance from Earth: 248 million miles (399 million km)

Average range: –225º to 63º F (–143º to 17º C)

Surface gravity: 0.377 that of Earth. A person weighing 80 pounds (36 kg) on Earth would weigh about 30 pounds (14 kg) on Mars.

Number of known moons: 2

How to Learn More about Mars

At the Library

Branley, Franklyn Mansfield. *Mission to Mars.* New York: HarperCollins, 2002.

Goss, Tim. *Mars.* Chicago: Heinemann Library, 2002.

Ride, Sally, and Tam O'Shaughnessy. *The Mystery of Mars.* New York: Crown, 1999.

Wunsch, Susi Trautmann. *The Adventures of Sojourner: The Mission to Mars that Thrilled the World.* New York: Mikaya Press, 1998.

On the Web

Visit our home page for lots of links about Mars:
http://www.childsworld.com/links.html
Note to Parents, Teachers, and Librarians: We routinely verify our Web links to make sure they're safe, active sites—so encourage your readers to check them out!

Through the Mail or by Phone

ADLER PLANETARIUM AND ASTRONOMY MUSEUM
1300 South Lake Shore Drive
Chicago, IL 60605-2403
312/922-STAR

NATIONAL AIR AND SPACE MUSEUM
7th and Independence Avenue, S.W.
Washington, DC 20560
202/357-2700

ROSE CENTER FOR EARTH AND SPACE
AMERICAN MUSEUM OF NATURAL HISTORY
Central Park West at 79th Street
New York, NY 10024-5192
212/769-5100

The Sun

Mercury

Venus

Earth

Mars

Jupiter

Saturn

Uranus

Neptune

Pluto

The solar system

Index

About the Author

Darlene R. Stille is a science writer. She has lived in Chicago, Illinois, all her life. When she was in high school, she fell in love with science. While attending the University of Illinois she discovered that she also loved writing. She was fortunate to find a career that allowed her to combine both her interests. Darlene Stille has written about 60 books for young people.